Mansfield

on old picture postcards

David Ottewell

1. A panoramic view of Mansfield from the Sand Hills on a postcard published anonymously and sent from the town in July 1917.

£3.95

INTRODUCTION

Although the first picture postcard in Britain was published in 1894, it was not until 1902 that the idea really caught on. The so-called "Golden Age" of postcards extended from then until the First World War, a period when cards were keenly bought both for sending and as pictures to collect.

Most of the illustrations in this book are from pre-1939 postcards, though a few show the town in the 1950s. Mansfield was well-covered by national publishers such as Valentine of Dundee or Francis Frith of Reigate, as well as area publishers from neighbouring towns – C. & A.G. Lewis of Nottingham and R. Sneath of Sheffield, for example – and local firms (G.S. Ellis, the Sherwood Photographic Co. and Ernest Gouk of Mansfield, and E. Osler of Forest town). The views are chosen to illustrate Mansfield in an earlier era. In some instances, buildings have now disappeared, in others the backgrounds remain while the events unfolding before them are changed in the forms of clothing, transport or advertising. The pictures combine to give us the opportunity to experience a walk down memory lane; a nostalgic reminder of things as they once were.

David Ottewell
July 1993

Designed and Published by
Reflections of a Bygone Age
Keyworth, Nottingham
1993

Printed by
Adlard Print and Typesetting Services,
Ruddington, Notts.

Acknowledgements: thanks to Maurice O'Connor for permission to use cards 34 and 36.

Front cover: Westgate about 1912 on a Boots photographic card, with the Oriental Cafe on the right. The pavements are piled high with deliveries, while a horse and cart belonging to the Great Central Railway monopolises the centre of the road. In the far distance on the left, beyond the pair of spectacles advertising an opticians, the spire of St. John's Church can just be seen.

Back Cover (top): Queen Street in the 1920s on a card by E.L. Scrivens of Doncaster.
(bottom): Nottingham Road, showing the two railway bridges.

ISBN 0 946245 79 7

2. Market Place on a 'Peveril Series' card, posted to Liversidge in Yorkshire in November 1915 by a soldier of no.18 Battalion based at nearby Clipstone Camp. The original market area of Mansfield was around the old cross on Westgate, but the site shown here was cleared for its present use between 1823 and 1845. The "Market" Hotel is on the left.

3. The thriving, bustling, market with its patchwork-quilt effect of stall coverings is regularly set up around the Bentinck Memorial. This was designed by T.C. Hine and built by C. Lindley in 1849, with the cost being met from public subscriptions. Postcard published by C. & A.G. Lewis of Nottingham as no. 523 in their long series of local views.

4. Lord George Bentinck was the son of the 4th Duke of Portland of nearby Welbeck Abbey. He died in 1848 whilst walking from his home to Thoresby Hall. Bentinck came to public attention initially as a race-horse owner and later as an M.P., proving to be a vociferous opponent of free trade. The gap in the monument was planned to hold a statue, but insufficient money was raised to complete the task. Card published locally by Gouk from a Chris Smith photo about 1905.

The Town Hall, Mansfield.

5. This postcard by Ernest Gouk of Mansfield reveals the Town Hall in all its splendour. Built in 1836 for £6,000, it contained Assembly Rooms as well as a library and newsroom. The card was posted to Norwich in August 1905: *"a view of the town Hall, which will give you a little idea of the Mansfield Centre",* wrote the sender.

MARKET STREET, MANSFIELD.

6. Market Street about 1930, featuring the railway viaduct, National Provincial Bank on the right, and Imperial Hairdressing Saloon on the left. No indication of who published the card.

7. Until the first half of the 19th century, this cross on Westgate marked the site of the town market; indeed, the cattle market continued to be held there until 1877. Notice the horse trough at the base of the cross. Postcard by Woolstone Bros in their 'Artlette' series, published about 1906.

8. This card in the Y.M.C.A. series gives something of a feel of earlier outdoor trading days in Westgate. Public announcements were also made from the cross, and it was here that in 1788 John Adams conducted the first Methodist service in Mansfield. Postcard sent to Maidstone in October 1917.

9. A quiet time on Westgate in 1913 captured on a postcard by Boots, and sent to Antwerp in Belgium. Two men can stop to chat in the road outside the plumber's showrooms, and there's a complete absence of motorised traffic. Note the clock outside Savage & Son's shop (which sold beers, wines and spirits). The tram lines down the centre of the street were laid for the route from Mansfield to Meden Square, Pleasley.

10. A tram with a Berry Hill Lane destination board rumbles down Westgate on a 'Peveril' Real Photo series card, sent to Felixstowe in July 1912. Horse droppings, one of the features of pre-WW1 streets, are prominent in the road.

11. Valentine's of Dundee postcard showing a much later (about 1937) view of Westgate looking in the opposite direction. "Ye Olde Eclipse" Hotel, selling Mansfield Ales, is on the left.

12. Two decades on, and another postcard by Valentine, posted at Mansfield in July 1956. British Home Stores is featured prominently on the left, and a straggle of market stalls are on the other side of the road. Compared to the previous view, some roofline changes can be seen beyond a new sign for Savage's.

FLOOD AT MANSFIELD
WEST GATE
MAY 30. 1912

13. Looking in the same direction, but in 1912, as an anonymous cameraman has captured a flooded Westgate after torrential storms on May 30th.

Westgate and Congregational Church, Mansfield.

14. The eminent Mansfield-born architect Watson Fothergill designed this ornate church for the congregationalists of the town. Built of local stone, it opened in 1878. The sender of the card comments *"I am sorry to say this P.C. is not very great. I could not get many nice views here."* Westend Bakery, owned by W.L. Renshaw, is to the right of this c.1916 card.

NOTTINGHAM ROAD, MANSFIELD

15. When the Cattle Market became too cumbersome to be held any longer in Westgate, it moved to this site on Nottingham Road on the edge of town. The open-topped tram features as the centrepiece of this Y.M.C.A. card, published about 1917.

16. Nottingham Road, Mansfield, with tramcar no.1 on its way to Berry Hill Lane. The "Plough" Inn is on the left of this photographic view card published by the Sherwood Photographic Company, Mansfield.

17. Further out of town, on Nottingham Road, car no.8 heads back to Mansfield. Postcard no.724 by C. and A.G. Lewis.

18. A policeman on point duty at the Leeming Street-Market Place junction. Redevelopment and road widening took place at the turn of the century here, giving better access to the town's principal shopping street. This card, published by Jackson & Son of Grimsby, was posted to Bishop Auckland in August 1925.

457.   Leeming Street, Mansfield.

19. Looking the opposite way down Leeming Street into the Market Place. The "Green Dragon" Hotel can be seen on the far right of this W.H. Smith postcard of about 1923. Arthur Holloway had recently become the new proprietor of the hotel, which was a popular meeting place until demolished in 1963.

S 10442   LEEMING STREET, MANSFIELD

20. Much further along Leeming Street was – and still is – the "Horse and Jockey" public house. The open-topped tram in the middle distance is just outside the Carnegie Library. Another W.H. Smith card, posted from Mansfield in November 1921.

21. The Scottish-American philanthropist Andrew Carnegie gave £3,500 for the building of this library on land donated by the Duke of Portland. Opened in 1905, it got a second-storey extension in 1932, and served until the Four Seasons Library replaced it in 1977. Postcard by Valentine, published about 1925.

22. Panoramic view of Church Street on a 1930s postcard.

S 5679 CHURCH ST. MANSFIELD.

23. This W.H. Smith card of about 1912 shows how pedestrians were able to wander about freely in Edwardian Mansfield: though the horse droppings in the street provide evidence of what transport there was. The railway viaduct dominates the street. The "Swan" Hotel is on the right: its narrow coach entrance was blocked up in 1910.

S 10452   THE SWAN HOTEL, MANSFIELD.

24. In centuries past, the "Swan" was one of the town's principal inns: a number of the local coaches and carriers began and terminated here. W.H. Smith postcard, sent to London in August 1916.

SWAN HOTEL
MANSFIELD

25. A "Swan" courtyard interior view on a card published by the Sherwood Photographic Company.

26. Valentine's card of the 1950s shows a busy scene in Church Street with the parish church of St. Peters central to the picture. It is the oldest of Mansfield's churches. H. Boole's butchers shop, the Leek and Moorland Building Society, and Margo's beauty salon are on the left.

27. An earlier view from the 1920s on a C. and A.G. Lewis postcard. W. Fox, house furnisher and cooper, and the Prudential Assurance Company are on the left.

E.L.S.220-1. St. Peter's Church, Mansfield.

28. The prolific Doncaster postcard firm of E.L. Scrivens published this view of St. Peter's Church about 1925. Built in a mixture of styles, the church is notable for its embattled roofline. The lower parts of the tower date from the 11th century, while the spire was added in 1669.

RAILWAY VIADUCT, MANSFIELD.

29. Seen on the card of Church Street *(illus.22),* the railway viaduct dominates the centre of Mansfield. Built with local stone from Langwith, this 15-arch viaduct was constructed in order to facilitate the extension of the Midland Railway's Nottingham-Mansfield railway to Worksop. The first passenger train travelled over it on 1st June 1875. Y.M.C.A. series card of about 1916.

30. Mansfield's Midland Station, a busy and thriving complex, provided services to Alfreton, Chesterfield, Newark, Nottingham, Worksop and Sutton-in-Ashfield at the time this 'HHH' series card was published. Incredibly, the town lost its railway services on 12th October 1964 when this station was closed to passenger traffic. Eight years earlier the town's other line, the Great Central, had its passenger services withdrawn.

MIDLAND STATION, MANSFIELD

31. A busy forecourt on this 1916 card in the Y.M.C.A. series with soldiers, possibly from Clipstone Camp, arriving in the cart. The first passenger train on the Midland service from Nottingham arrived at this station on 9th October 1849.

32. Mansfield Woodhouse on the Midland line 1¹/2 miles north of the town's station, seen on this Edwardian postcard. The Midland Hotel is advertised on a hoarding on the platform.

33. A Valentine's card sent to Ambergate in August 1908 shows an open-topped tram making its way up Chesterfield Road into Mansfield from Pleasley. This was the first route on the local tramway system, opening on 11th July 1905. The journey took 11 minutes and cost 3d.

34. Known as the Mansfield and District Traction Co., the tramway system was originally owned by local shareholders before being acquired by Balfour Beatty. The system covered 12.28 miles and ran a total of 30 trams. This photographic card by M.J. O'Connor, dating from 1931, shows car 28 which was sold to Sunderland Corporation the following year and ran there until 1954.

35. Tram no.1 looking a bit worse for wear after a crash. Mr. H.M. Wharmby is sat on its front. In the early days, trams on occasions went out of control either down Stockwell Gate, Leeming Street or Skerry Hill.

36. Both open and closed top trams operated on the five routes from Mansfield (to Pleasley, Huthwaite, Mansfield Woodhouse, Crown Farm and Nottingham Road/Berry Hill Lane). The last tram ran in 1932, by which time it is estimated that in 27 years the service had carried 134 million passengers. Tram no. 20, seen here in 1931 at Mansfield's Market Place, was a second-hand car purchased from a tramway company near Belfast. Another photographic card by M.J. O'Connnor.

St. John's Church and School, Mansfield.

37. The church of St. John was constructed in 1856. In the foreground can be seen St. John's School, built with local stone. Anonymously-published card from about 1906.

St. Mark's Church, Mansfield

38. The expansion of Mansfield at the end of the last century resulted in a need for more places of worship. St. Mark's Church was built on Nottingham Road and opened in 1896. Postcard by Valentine, posted from Mansfield in July 1912.

S.10450   ST. LAURENCE'S CHURCH, SKERRY HILL, MANSFIELD.

39. St. Lawrence's Church at Skerry Hill was also part of the religious expansion programme at the turn of the century, being opened in September 1909. Initially it was under St. Peter's control but it achieved full parish status in 1921. This W.H. Smith postcard, sent to Louth in December 1919, comments *"this is the last card I shall send you while I am a soldier".*

Catholic Church, Mansfield.
Rex Series. 1132.

40. St. Philip's Catholic Church on Chesterfield Road was opened in March 1925. For the preceding 50 years, the Catholic community had worshipped on Ratcliffe Gate. The sign advertises a garden fete in High Oakham Park on 27th July with Pleasley Colliery Prize Band as the star attraction. Card in the 'Rex' series (no.1132), published in the late 1920s, and posted to Newark in May 1929.

Ellis, Photo.　　　WESLEYAN CHAPEL, MANSFIELD.　　*Willman, Publisher.*

41. Bridge Street Wesleyan Church is still standing today, an impressive building incorporating local materials. This early postcard, published by Willman, was sent to Sheffield in October 1903.

THE CEMETERY CHAPEL. MANSFIELD

LILYWHITE LTD.
TRIANGLE. HALIFAX.

42. The cemetery chapel was opened in December 1857 at a cost of £7,250. The card by Lilywhite of Halifax shows the two mortuary chapels linked by an archway surmounted by a tower with an octagonal spire. This contained a mausoleum belonging to the family of Sir Edward S. Walker.

Thompson's Grave, Mansfield,

G.2801.

43. Local benefactor Charles Thompson lived from 1714 to 1784. He had a varied life travelling the world, including acting as an agent for Russian merchants in Persia and surviving the great earthquake of 1755 in Lisbon. Mansfield, however, was his chosen resting place.

Boys' Grammar School, Mansfield

44. Though the school was founded in 1561, these new buildings for Queen Elizabeth's Boys Grammar School were opened on Chesterfield Road in 1878. Costing £1,000, they were designed by Giles and Gough of London. The first headmaster in the new buildings was the Reverend Edwin Johnson. Valentine's series card, sent from Mansfield in May 1915.

The Girls Grammar School, Mansfield

45. Another Valentine card showing the Queen Elizabeth Girls School off Woodhouse Road. It was built on land purchased from the Brunts' Charity. Q.E.G.S. moved into these new buildings in 1891, and there have been many additions and alterations during the present century.

BRUNTS SCHOOL, MANSFIELD   G 9847

46. Although the foundation stone was only laid in 1893, Brunts Technical School can trace its origins back a further century. The Thompson's School *(see illus. 42 for reference)* on Toothill Lane opened in 1787, and it combined with the Brunts Charity to form this school. These buildings on Woodhouse Road closed in 1987 and at present stand sadly neglected.

47. High Oakham School on 'Rex' series postcard no. 1124, posted at Mansfield in October 1930. The sender points out the pillar box (by the trees) and the tram tracks. The building, on Nottingham Road near the point where the trams turned off for Berry Hill terminus, is now a middle school.

48. Borough architect R. Frank Vallance designed Rosemary School, the first elementary school in Mansfield: the first pupils arrived on 1st May 1899, and it was officially opened by Lord Belper in the following year. It closed in July 1977. Postcard by Lilywhite of Halifax.

49. Carr Bank house and grounds were purchased by the council from the 6th Duke of Portland after the first world war. In 1924 the war memorial (right, in distance) was unveiled, and the grounds turned into a park, dedicated to the men who gave their lives. The house (centre) had originally been built for Charles Stanton, a local cotton spinner, but he sold it to the 4th Duke of Portland. From 1836-1907 it was leased to the Greenhalgh family, millowners *(see illus. 57)*. After the council bought the house, it was used first for the College of Art, but was later converted to council offices. This card was published by Valentine in the late 1930s.

50. The Technical College on Chesterfield Road was opened in October 1928 by Lord Chelmsford. Two years later, the School of Art took up residence at the rear. Note the tram lines in the centre of the picture on this anonymously-published postcard.

S 2377   CHESTERFIELD ROAD, MANSFIELD.

51. A very empty Chesterfield Road on a W.H. Smith card postally used in September 1915. A solitary horse and cart is carefully avoiding the tram lines, while the two men on the left with a horse are standing at the Clumber Street-Westhill Drive junction. The house behind them marks the site of the College of Art. *"I am having a nice time here",* wrote Clarice, *"I don't want to come back to business any more".*

Titchfield Park, Mansfield. No. 723.

52. The area originally known as Water Meadows (a name recently revived in the town) belonged to the Duke of Portland, who gave it to the townspeople in 1914 to celebrate the coming of age of his son the Marquis of Titchfield – hence the park's name. This card by C. and A.G. Lewis shows the tank which arrived by train, having been sent as a thankyou for the large sums of money raised in Mansfield on national savings during the 1914-18 war. The tank, no.255, was put on show in the park after a ceremony in May 1919. This postcard was not actually used until March 1931: *"You go through this park to Mansfield, very pretty now with the spring flowers",* wrote the sender.

53. The General Hospital on the Westhill Drive site began life as a 5-bed hospital opened by the Duke of Portland on 27th October 1890. Many extensions have since been carried out but the site remains too small and much of its work has been transferred to King's Mill. Card published by Valentine in the 1930s.

54. Ransom Sanitorium was opened on Ratcher Hill in 1902 to specialise in the treatment of tuberculosis and other chest complaints. Valentine's card of c.1908 vintage.

55. The Rock Houses, Mansfield, on C. and A.G. Lewis card no.535. At one time, up to twelve families occupied dwellings in the caves: an uncomfortable living arrangement, but possibly the best that some local destitute families could manage.

56. This card, sent from Mansfield to Alford in September 1905, shows John Bramwell outside the last occupied Rock House. John died in 1900, and his wife Charlotte had moved out by 1905.

MANSFIELD COLLIERY, FOREST TOWN.

57. E. Osler of Forest Town published this card of Mansfield Colliery, which was sent by Bolsover Colliery Company in 1903. Conditions were very spartan, and it wasn't until May 1936 that the pit-head baths were opened. The card was posted to Coventry in August 1920.

FIELD MILL
MANSFELD JWS.

58. Field Mill was built at the end of the 18th century by the Duke of Portland, and for many years the mill was leased to the Greenhalgh family. A fire in 1901 led to it falling in disuse, and it was demolished in 1925, with its giant 40-foot diameter wheel surviving until 1940. Photographic card, sent to Leeds in September 1904.

59. Thomas Walker, a former High Sheriff of Nottinghamshire, owned Berry Hill Hall initially, before it was sold to the Hollins family, employers of local labour at their textile mills in nearby Pleasley Vale. Card published by the Sherwood Photographic Co.

60. In May 1924 the Hall became a miners' convalescent home and remained so until 1951, when it was taken over by the National Health Service. Empire View Productions published this card about 1926.

61. A rural view of Berry Hill, though this card is as recent as the 1950s, and provides a reminder of how much green belt has been lost since then. Valentine's 'Sepiatype' series card.

62. A packed tram at the crossroads at Crown Farm terminus. Miners are returning home after a shift at the local colliery. The postcard was sent to Loughborough in August 1911.

63. The tram coming down the hill on Yorke Street is on the Mansfield Woodhouse route. The large building to the left next to the shop with its advertising signs is the Central Mines Rescue Centre opened in 1912. C. and A.G. Lewis card no. 2754.

64. Built about 1790, the water-powered Reed Mill was situated on Cauldwell Brook, which was a tributary of the River Maun. It was demolished in 1971.

S 10436 · DEBDALE LANE, MANSFIELD.

65. Debdale Lane in 1912 on a W.H. Smith postcard. This rural scene between Mansfield Woodhouse and Skegby has not changed much.

66. Debdale Hall, built in the 18th century, was for many years the home of the Talbot-Coke family. In February 1948 it opened as a Recovery Hospital, and is now a grade II listed building. Card by Sherwood Photographic Co.

67. Valentine-published card of Stockwell Gate, with the Star Tea Company premises on the right, flanked by an archway belonging to the Portland Temperance Hotel, and to the left by Peak's stores. The card dates from c.1920.

68. A 1930s view of Stockwell Gate, with Taylor's wine merchants and Barclays Bank on the right.

69. Two decades later, on a Frith-published card, there are more pedestrians and a number of parked cars.

70. The earliest of this quartet of Stockwell Gate cards shows the Market Place end. The "Black Horse" Inn is on the right; in 1905, when this 'Jay-em-Jay' series card (Jackson & Son, Grimsby) was published, the proprietor was T.H. Harper. He was in competition with eleven other inns on Stockwell Gate alone!

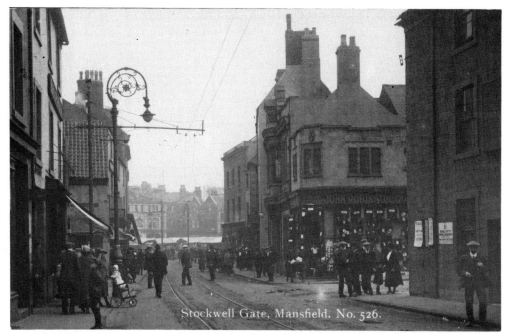

Stockwell Gate, Mansfield. No. 526.

71. A lively street scene on a C. & A.G. Lewis card of about 1920 showing prominently the premises of John Robinson & Son, general outfitters. Notice the ornate top of the lampholder, and below it, the pushchair about to cross the road.

COPYRIGHT
MFD. 30.

BULL FARM, MANSFIELD.

LILYWHITE LTD.
TRIANGLE HALIFAX.

72. As the population of Mansfield increased, so did the need for more housing. This resulted in a large building programme on the outskirts of town, including at Bull Farm, as seen on this Lilywhite postcard from the mid-1920s.

73. Bleak Hills, Mansfield, on a card by Montgomery of Nottingham. This area is on the Nottingham side of town in the Field Mill direction.

74. Woodhouse Road had been the chosen site for the Brunts School and the Girls Grammar School. A little further out, housing was taking up the available land.

75. A superbly-animated street scene of the Old Cross in the centre of Mansfield Woodhouse. The postcard was sent to Leicester in March 1911 by someone who was staying at Debdale Hall with a new baby.

76. Five for the price of one! G.S. Ellis postcard featuring different individual designs: Woodhouse Road, Yeomans Hills, The Cross, Market Place (with tram) and, in the centre, St. Edmund's Church.

77. Mansfield Wood-house Hospital on a photographic card sent to Nuneaton in July 1904.

78. St. Edmund's Church and the "Castle" at Mansfield Woodhouse on a G.S. Ellis card.

CHURCH & CASTLE MANSFIELD WOODHOUSE. "THOMAS"

Cyclists Hostel, Mansfield Woodhouse.   G.2806

79. Valentine's series postcard showing the cyclist's hostel.

80. Mansfield Mechanics football team, charity cup winners in 1905. Postcard published by Ellis.

MANSFIELD SALVATION ARMY BAND. 1940

81. Most towns had their own Salvation Army band in the first half of this century. This card features the Mansfield group in 1940.